Sikhi

This book belongs to

_____

www.pegasusforkids.com

Published by Kuldeep Jain for B. Jain Publishers (P) Ltd., D-157, Sector 63, Noida - 201307, U.P

Printed in India

This graded series is written in easy-to-understand English. The aim is to develop reading habit in children and to increase their vocabulary.

Sikhism is one of the youngest religions in the world. The Sikh religion dates back to the 15th century and was founded by Guru Nanak.

The religion is based on teachings of Guru Nanak and those of the nine gurus that followed him.

Though Sikhism finds its roots in Hinduism, Sikhism does not believe in idol worship. It is a religion that firmly believes in the idea of One God.

It is also a religion that firmly believes that people of different races or religions are equal in the eyes of God. More than religious rituals, Sikhism stresses on leading an honest life by focusing on selflessly serving and caring for others.

Guru Nanak, the founder of Sikhism, is said to have been born in April 1469 near Lahore (a city in present day Pakistan). From a very young age he began questioning Hindu and Muslim religious customs.

He felt that these religions put too much importance on rituals. He was against the caste system and even as a boy, Nanak refused to take part in the Hindu sacred thread ceremony.

Nanak's early years were dotted by many events that proved that he was different and special.

Nanak was a keen learner in school and began writing spiritually inspired compositions. Though Nanak married and took on household responsibilities, Nanak continued his charitable ways. He would spend all his earnings on feeding the poor.

Nanak soon met a Muslim minstrel named Mardana. They met every day near a river, where they meditated before going to work. One morning, Nanak walked into the river and disappeared into the water.

Everyone assumed that he had drowned. But after three days, Nanak emerged from the river. People realised that Nanak had gained enlightenment and began to call him 'Guru'.

After this Nanak gave up his life as a householder. Nanak along with Mardana became a travelling minstrel. Mardana played a stringed instrument to which Nanak sang his compositions praising and spreading the idea of One God.

Over a period of 25 years, they made 5 long, tough journeys, spreading the idea of One God.

Nanak developed Sikhism denouncing idol worship. His teachings stressed on daily worship and expressing faith through meditation. A key idea of Sikhism was selfless service and the sharing of honest earnings.

Nanak set about abolishing the hierarchy of caste. He established ideals of equality for women and spoke against blind practices of rituals.

Nanak wrote 7,500 lines of verses which were later included in the scripture of the Guru Granth Sahib. He dedicated his life to travel with the aim

of sharing his new found philosophy. Guru Nanak passed on his enlightened leadership of this new religion to nine successive Gurus: Guru Angad, Guru Amar Das, Guru Ram Das, Guru Arjan, Guru Hargobind, Guru Har Rai, Guru Harkrishan, Guru Tegh Bahadur and Guru Gobind Singh.

The tenth and last Sikh guru, Guru Gobind Singh formed the Khalsa (the pure) order, the order of the Soldier-Saints.

In 1699, on the day of Baisakhi festival, Guru Gobind Singh stood before a huge crowd with a sword and asked any one of them to offer their heads to him. Only five men of different caste volunteered to get their heads cut off.

But the Guru did not cut their heads off. Instead, the five men were led in front of the gathering, dressed in new clothes their heads covered with neatly tied turbans, with swords dangling by their sides.

Those five Sikhs were the first to be initiated into the Khalsa. Guru Gobind Singh called them Panj Piare (the five beloved of the Guru).

23

The Sikhs introduced to the Khalsa order also vowed to wear the five physical symbols representing the Khalsa. These symbols were uncut hair and beard, a comb, a steel bracelet, short breeches and a sword.

Guru Gobind Singh was himself initiated as their guru by the five disciples, and had his name changed from Gobind Rai to Gobind Singh.

Guru Gobind Singh also decreed an end to the line of gurus. The writings of all the 10 gurus were then put together into one book, which is known as Guru Granth Sahib.

Guru Gobind Singh declared the Sikh holy book as his successor. Sikhs give it the same status and respect as a human guru. The three duties that a Sikh must carry out are pray, work and give.

A key aspect of the religion is the idea of langar or community kitchens that provide free meals for devotees and other people who come to the gurudwara (the Sikh place of worship). The free kitchen operates entirely through voluntary service (seva).

Strict hygiene is maintained while cooking this food. The food is vegetarian. This concept is in keeping with the idea of selfless service that is an important idea in Sikhism.

Sikhism Fact File

- There are said to be close to 20 million followers of Sikhism in the world.

- The most significant religious centre for the Sikhs is the Golden Temple at Amritsar in the state of Punjab, India.

- The Sikh code of conduct and conventions is outlined in a document called the Sikh Rehat Maryada. It is based on the norms established by the teachings of the 10 Sikh gurus.

- Gurdwaras display a saffron-coloured triangular flag bearing the symbol of the Sikh faith. This flag is called the Nishan Sahib.

Vocabulary

youngest   instrument

idol   minstrel

rituals   denouncing

selflessly   enlightened

founder   turbans

sacred   bracelet

spiritually   breeches

compositions   decreed

Activity

Help your child comprehend the story and develop an understanding of values of life through the experiences of the characters. Ask them questions and encourage them to think, ponder and seek answers. This will trigger their critical thinking, creativity and curiosity.

1. Who is the founder of Sikhism?
2. How did Guru Nanak receive enlightnment?
3. How did Guru Gobind Singh redefine Sikhism?
4. What is langar?